Copyright © 2023 by Cameron Bailey (Author)

All rights reserved. No part of this book may be reproduced or utilized in any form or by any means, electronic or mechanical, including photocopying, recording or by any information storage and retrieval system, without permission in writing from the publisher, except for brief quotations in critical articles or reviews.

The content of this book is based on various sources and is intended for educational and entertainment purposes only. While the author has made every effort to ensure the accuracy, completeness, and reliability of the information provided, the information may be subject to errors, omissions, or inaccuracies. Therefore, the author makes no warranties, express or implied, regarding the content of this book.

Readers are advised to seek the guidance of a licensed professional before attempting any techniques or actions outlined in this book. The author is not responsible for any losses, damages, or injuries that may arise from the use of information contained within. The information provided in this book is not intended to be a substitute for professional advice, and readers should not rely solely on the information presented.

By reading this book, readers acknowledge that the author is not providing legal, financial, medical, or professional advice. Any reliance on the information contained in this book is solely at the reader's own risk.

Thank you for selecting this book as a valuable source of knowledge and inspiration. Our aim is to provide you with insights and information that will enrich your understanding and enhance your personal growth. We appreciate your decision to embark on this journey of discovery with us, and we hope that this book will exceed your expectations and leave a lasting impact on your life.

Title: Triumphs of Self-Confidence
Subtitle: Inspiring Stories of Overcoming Doubt and Achieving Success

Series: The Secrets of Self-Confidence: A Comprehensive Guide to Achieving Your Goals
Author: Cameron Bailey

Table of Contents

Introduction **5**
What is self-confidence? *5*
Why is it important to read inspiring stories of self-confidence? *7*
How to read inspiring stories of self-confidence *9*

Chapter 1: The importance of reading inspiring stories of self-confidence **11**
Self-confidence is essential for a happy and successful life *11*
When you have self-confidence, you are more likely to take risks, achieve your goals, and be happy with your life *14*
Reading inspiring stories of self-confidence can help you boost your own self-confidence *17*

Chapter 2: How to read inspiring stories of self-confidence **20**
Find stories that resonate with you *20*
Read the stories with an open mind *22*
Pay attention to the details *24*
Reflect on the stories *26*

Chapter 3: Inspiring stories of self-confidence **28**
The story of Malala Yousafzai *28*
The story of Oprah Winfrey *31*

The story of Nelson Mandela *33*
The story of Helen Keller *36*
The story of Stephen Hawking *39*

Chapter 4: How to use inspiring stories of self-confidence to boost your own self-confidence....... 42

Remember that you are not alone *42*
Set goals for yourself *44*
Take action *46*
Believe in yourself *49*

Chapter 5: How to find, share, and benefit from inspiring stories of self-confidence 52

Finding inspiring stories of self-confidence *52*
Sharing inspiring stories of self-confidence with others *55*
The benefits of reading inspiring stories of self-confidence *59*

Conclusion **62**

The importance of self-confidence *62*
How to boost your self-confidence *64*

Wordbook **69**
Supplementary Materials **71**

Introduction
What is self-confidence?

Self-confidence is a crucial aspect of our mental and emotional well-being. It is defined as the belief in oneself, one's abilities, and one's judgment. When you have self-confidence, you feel capable, competent, and worthy. You trust your own abilities and have faith in your decisions.

Self-confidence is not a fixed trait; it is a learned behavior that can be developed and improved over time. It involves a combination of factors, such as our past experiences, our upbringing, our personality, and our mindset.

One of the key components of self-confidence is self-esteem. Self-esteem is the overall evaluation of ourselves and our worth. It is how we feel about ourselves and our abilities. When we have high self-esteem, we are more likely to have high self-confidence.

Another factor that influences self-confidence is our mindset. People with a growth mindset believe that they can learn and improve their abilities over time. They see challenges as opportunities to learn and grow. On the other hand, people with a fixed mindset believe that their abilities are fixed and cannot be improved. They see challenges as threats to their self-worth.

Self-confidence is important because it affects many aspects of our lives, including our relationships, our career, and our overall happiness. People with high self-confidence are more likely to take risks, set goals, and persevere in the face of challenges. They are also more likely to be successful in their endeavors and have fulfilling relationships.

However, low self-confidence can be detrimental to our well-being. It can lead to negative self-talk, self-doubt, and self-sabotage. It can prevent us from taking risks, trying new things, and pursuing our goals.

In summary, self-confidence is the belief in oneself, one's abilities, and one's judgment. It can be developed and improved over time through factors such as self-esteem, mindset, and experiences. Self-confidence is crucial for our well-being, affecting many aspects of our lives. It is important to cultivate self-confidence to achieve success and happiness.

Why is it important to read inspiring stories of self-confidence?

Self-confidence is an essential aspect of our lives that affects our relationships, career, and overall well-being. When we lack self-confidence, we may doubt our abilities and avoid taking risks, which can prevent us from achieving our goals and living fulfilling lives. However, reading inspiring stories of self-confidence can be a powerful tool to boost our own self-confidence and achieve success.

Firstly, reading inspiring stories of self-confidence can provide us with role models who have overcome self-doubt and achieved great things. These stories can inspire us to take action and pursue our goals, even when faced with challenges or setbacks. They can also help us see that we are not alone in our struggles and that it is possible to overcome our doubts and fears.

Secondly, reading inspiring stories of self-confidence can help us develop a growth mindset, which is essential for building self-confidence. People with a growth mindset believe that their abilities can be improved with effort and practice, and they see challenges as opportunities to learn and grow. When we read stories of people who have overcome challenges and achieved success, we can adopt a growth mindset and develop the belief that we too can improve our abilities.

Thirdly, reading inspiring stories of self-confidence can help us reframe our negative self-talk and self-doubt. When we read stories of people who have faced similar challenges and overcome them, we can challenge our own negative beliefs and replace them with positive ones. We can start to see ourselves as capable and worthy, and we can develop a more positive and optimistic outlook on life.

Finally, reading inspiring stories of self-confidence can provide us with practical tips and strategies to build our own self-confidence. These stories can teach us how to overcome obstacles, take risks, and develop a positive mindset. They can also provide us with a sense of hope and motivation to keep going, even when faced with setbacks.

In conclusion, reading inspiring stories of self-confidence is essential for building our own self-confidence and achieving success. These stories can provide us with role models, develop a growth mindset, reframe our negative self-talk, and provide us with practical tips and strategies. By reading inspiring stories of self-confidence, we can overcome our doubts and fears and live fulfilling and successful lives.

How to read inspiring stories of self-confidence

Reading inspiring stories of self-confidence can be a powerful tool to boost our own self-confidence and achieve success. However, it is important to know how to read these stories effectively to get the most out of them. Here are some tips on how to read inspiring stories of self-confidence:

1. Find stories that resonate with you: The first step in reading inspiring stories of self-confidence is to find stories that resonate with you. Look for stories of people who have overcome challenges or setbacks that are similar to the ones you are facing. By finding stories that you can relate to, you will be more likely to feel inspired and motivated to take action.

2. Read the stories with an open mind: When reading inspiring stories of self-confidence, it is important to approach them with an open mind. Avoid any preconceived notions or biases that may prevent you from fully absorbing the story. Be open to learning new perspectives and ideas, and allow yourself to be inspired by the story.

3. Pay attention to the details: When reading inspiring stories of self-confidence, pay attention to the details. Look for the specific actions that the person took to overcome their challenges or achieve their goals. Take note of any strategies or tips that the person used to build their self-

confidence. By paying attention to these details, you can learn from the experiences of others and apply these lessons to your own life.

4. Reflect on the stories: After reading inspiring stories of self-confidence, take some time to reflect on what you have learned. Think about how the story applies to your own life and how you can use the lessons from the story to improve your self-confidence. Consider journaling about your thoughts and reflections to solidify your learnings.

By following these tips, you can effectively read inspiring stories of self-confidence and use them to build your own self-confidence. Remember that each story is unique, and there is no one-size-fits-all approach to reading these stories. Find what works best for you and use these stories to inspire and motivate you to achieve your own success.

Chapter 1: The importance of reading inspiring stories of self-confidence

Self-confidence is essential for a happy and successful life

Self-confidence is a crucial element in achieving a happy and successful life. It is the belief in oneself and one's abilities to succeed and overcome challenges. Self-confidence enables individuals to take risks, face new challenges, and pursue their goals with determination and resilience. In this section, we will explore the importance of self-confidence for a happy and successful life.

First and foremost, self-confidence plays a vital role in personal happiness. When individuals have self-confidence, they feel more secure and comfortable in their own skin. They are less likely to compare themselves to others or seek validation from external sources. Instead, they find joy and fulfillment in their own accomplishments and progress towards their goals. This leads to greater feelings of satisfaction and happiness in life.

Additionally, self-confidence is essential for building healthy relationships. When individuals have self-confidence, they are more likely to communicate effectively, assert their boundaries, and show respect towards others. This leads to more positive interactions and deeper connections with loved ones, friends, and colleagues. Conversely, individuals who lack self-confidence may struggle with communication, have difficulty asserting their needs, and may be prone to self-doubt and insecurity. This can lead to strained relationships and isolation.

Furthermore, self-confidence is a critical factor in achieving success. When individuals have self-confidence, they are more likely to set ambitious goals and pursue them with determination. They are less likely to be deterred by setbacks or failures and are more resilient in the face of challenges. This enables them to persevere through difficult times and achieve their desired outcomes.

On the other hand, individuals who lack self-confidence may struggle to set ambitious goals, may give up easily in the face of challenges, or may struggle to overcome setbacks. This can limit their potential for success and lead to feelings of disappointment and dissatisfaction.

In conclusion, self-confidence is essential for a happy and successful life. It enables individuals to feel secure and comfortable in their own skin, build healthy relationships, and achieve their goals with determination and resilience. By reading inspiring stories of self-confidence and learning from the experiences of others, individuals can build and strengthen their own self-confidence, leading to a more fulfilling and successful life.

When you have self-confidence, you are more likely to take risks, achieve your goals, and be happy with your life

Self-confidence is a crucial factor in achieving success and happiness in life. It enables individuals to take risks, pursue their goals with determination, and find fulfillment in their accomplishments. In this section, we will explore the relationship between self-confidence and achievement.

When individuals have self-confidence, they are more likely to take risks. They are willing to step outside their comfort zones, try new things, and pursue opportunities that may be challenging or intimidating. This willingness to take risks enables individuals to grow, learn, and achieve things they may not have thought possible. They are also more likely to seize opportunities and make the most of their potential.

For example, consider an individual who lacks self-confidence and is hesitant to speak up in meetings or pitch their ideas to their boss. This individual may miss out on opportunities to showcase their talents, build relationships with colleagues, and advance their career. On the other hand, an individual with self-confidence may be more likely to speak up, share their ideas, and take on new challenges. This may lead to recognition, promotion, and greater fulfillment in their work.

Moreover, self-confidence is essential for achieving goals. When individuals have self-confidence, they are more likely to set ambitious goals and pursue them with determination. They believe in their ability to succeed and are less likely to be deterred by setbacks or obstacles. This enables them to persevere through challenges and achieve their desired outcomes.

For instance, consider an individual who lacks self-confidence and is hesitant to pursue a new career path. This individual may doubt their abilities, feel intimidated by the challenges, and ultimately give up on their aspirations. On the other hand, an individual with self-confidence may be more likely to pursue their career goals, even if they face challenges or setbacks along the way. This determination and resilience enable them to achieve their goals and find fulfillment in their career.

Finally, self-confidence is closely linked to happiness. When individuals have self-confidence, they are more likely to be satisfied with their lives and find fulfillment in their accomplishments. They are less likely to compare themselves to others, seek validation from external sources, or feel inadequate. Instead, they find joy and happiness in their own progress and achievements.

For example, consider an individual who lacks self-confidence and constantly compares themselves to others. This individual may feel inadequate, constantly striving to meet unrealistic standards or seeking validation from others. On the other hand, an individual with self-confidence may be more likely to focus on their own progress and accomplishments, finding joy and fulfillment in their own journey.

In conclusion, self-confidence is essential for taking risks, achieving goals, and finding happiness in life. By reading inspiring stories of self-confidence and learning from the experiences of others, individuals can build and strengthen their own self-confidence, leading to a more fulfilling and successful life.

Reading inspiring stories of self-confidence can help you boost your own self-confidence

Reading inspiring stories of self-confidence can be an effective way to boost your own self-confidence. When you read about others who have overcome obstacles and achieved success, it can help you to believe in your own abilities and potential. In this section, we will explore how reading inspiring stories of self-confidence can help you boost your own self-confidence.

1. Provides a Role Model When you read inspiring stories of self-confidence, you are learning from real-life examples of people who have overcome challenges and achieved success. These people can serve as role models for you, showing you what is possible when you believe in yourself and persevere through difficult times.

2. Encourages Positive Thinking Reading inspiring stories of self-confidence can help you to focus on the positive aspects of your own life. Instead of dwelling on your shortcomings and failures, you can shift your focus to the positive steps you have taken and the progress you have made. This positive thinking can help to build your self-confidence and motivation to keep moving forward.

3. Offers a Fresh Perspective Sometimes, when we are feeling stuck or discouraged, we can benefit from a fresh

perspective. Reading inspiring stories of self-confidence can offer you that perspective. By learning from the experiences of others, you can gain new insights and ideas for how to approach your own challenges and achieve your goals.

4. Helps You to Overcome Self-Doubt Self-doubt is one of the biggest obstacles to building self-confidence. When you read inspiring stories of self-confidence, you can see how others have faced their own self-doubt and overcome it. This can help you to recognize your own self-doubt and find strategies to overcome it.

5. Offers Practical Advice Many inspiring stories of self-confidence offer practical advice and strategies for building self-confidence. By reading about what has worked for others, you can apply those strategies to your own life and start building your own self-confidence.

6. Helps You to Feel Empowered Finally, reading inspiring stories of self-confidence can make you feel empowered. When you see how others have overcome challenges and achieved their goals, it can give you a sense of empowerment and motivation to take action in your own life. This feeling of empowerment can be a powerful catalyst for building your own self-confidence.

In conclusion, reading inspiring stories of self-confidence can be an effective way to boost your own self-confidence. By providing role models, encouraging positive thinking, offering a fresh perspective, helping you to overcome self-doubt, offering practical advice, and making you feel empowered, these stories can help you to build the self-confidence you need to achieve your goals and live a happy and successful life.

Chapter 2: How to read inspiring stories of self-confidence

Find stories that resonate with you

Finding stories that resonate with you is an essential step in reading inspiring stories of self-confidence. When you read a story that resonates with you, it means that you can relate to the experience of the person in the story. This connection helps you to feel inspired and motivated to build your own self-confidence.

Here are some tips for finding stories that resonate with you:

1. Look for stories that reflect your own experiences: If you have struggled with self-confidence in the past, look for stories of people who have faced similar challenges and overcome them. For example, if you are a shy person, you may want to look for stories of people who were once shy but have since built their confidence.

2. Choose stories about people you admire: You may have a role model or someone you look up to. Look for stories about their journey to self-confidence. Reading about someone you admire can inspire you to follow in their footsteps.

3. Read a variety of stories: Don't limit yourself to stories that are similar to your own experience or about

people you admire. Explore different stories and experiences to broaden your understanding of self-confidence. You may be surprised at how much you can learn from a story that is vastly different from your own.

4. Use online resources: There are many websites and blogs that feature inspiring stories of self-confidence. Use these resources to find stories that resonate with you. You can also find stories on social media platforms like Instagram or Twitter by using hashtags like #selfconfidence or #inspiration.

Once you have found stories that resonate with you, take the time to reflect on them. Think about how the person in the story overcame their self-doubt and what strategies they used to build their confidence. Use this information to create a plan for building your own self-confidence.

Remember, finding stories that resonate with you is a personal journey. Take your time and explore different stories until you find the ones that inspire you the most.

Read the stories with an open mind

When reading inspiring stories of self-confidence, it's important to approach them with an open mind. This means being receptive to new ideas and perspectives, even if they challenge your existing beliefs.

Here are some tips on how to read inspiring stories with an open mind:

1. Let go of your preconceptions: It's easy to approach a story with a set of expectations or assumptions. However, these preconceptions can prevent you from truly engaging with the material. Try to let go of any preconceived notions and approach the story with an open mind.

2. Be curious: Curiosity is a powerful tool for learning and growth. As you read the story, be curious about the experiences and insights being shared. Ask yourself questions like, "What can I learn from this?" or "How might this apply to my own life?"

3. Suspend judgment: When reading inspiring stories, it's important to suspend judgment and avoid jumping to conclusions. Remember that everyone's experiences and perspectives are unique, and what works for one person may not work for another.

4. Pay attention to emotions: Reading inspiring stories can be an emotional experience. Pay attention to how

you're feeling as you read. Are you feeling inspired, challenged, or motivated? Are there any emotions that are blocking your ability to engage with the story?

5. Practice empathy: Empathy is the ability to understand and share the feelings of others. When reading inspiring stories, try to put yourself in the shoes of the person who is sharing their experiences. This can help you better understand their perspective and relate to their journey.

Overall, reading inspiring stories with an open mind can help you gain new insights and perspectives, and ultimately boost your own self-confidence. So, approach each story with curiosity and empathy, and be willing to learn and grow from the experiences being shared.

Pay attention to the details

When reading inspiring stories of self-confidence, it's important to pay attention to the details. This means not only reading the surface level events of the story, but also analyzing the deeper meaning and lessons that can be learned. By paying attention to the details, you can fully understand the message the author is trying to convey and how it applies to your own life. Here are some tips on how to pay attention to the details:

1. Look for themes: When reading a story, look for recurring themes or ideas. These themes can provide insight into the author's message and what they want you to take away from the story.

2. Identify the turning point: In every good story, there is a turning point where the main character faces a challenge or obstacle. Identify this turning point and analyze how the character overcame it. This can provide inspiration for how you can overcome obstacles in your own life.

3. Examine the character's mindset: Pay attention to the thoughts and feelings of the main character throughout the story. This can give you insight into how the character was able to overcome self-doubt and build self-confidence.

4. Note the language and tone: The language and tone used in a story can also provide clues about the author's

message. Look for words and phrases that convey a sense of determination, strength, and resilience.

5. Connect the story to your own life: As you read the story, think about how the events and themes relate to your own life. Are there any lessons or insights that you can apply to your own journey towards self-confidence?

By paying attention to these details, you can fully immerse yourself in the story and gain a deeper understanding of how it relates to building self-confidence. Remember to take notes and reflect on what you've learned, as this can help solidify the lessons and make them easier to apply to your own life.

Reflect on the stories

Reflection is an important part of reading and learning from inspiring stories of self-confidence. It allows us to gain a deeper understanding of the story and how it can be applied to our own lives. Here are some ways to reflect on the stories:

1. Journaling: One of the best ways to reflect on the stories is to write about them in a journal. This allows you to record your thoughts and feelings about the story, as well as any insights or lessons you may have gained from it. When reflecting on a story, try to focus on specific details or moments that stood out to you, and consider why they resonated with you.

2. Discussion: Discussing the stories with others can also be a great way to reflect on them. You can talk about your own interpretations of the story, as well as how it relates to your own experiences. You may also gain new insights from hearing other people's perspectives.

3. Visualization: Another way to reflect on the stories is to visualize the events as they unfold in your mind. This can help you to better understand the emotions and motivations of the characters, as well as how the story relates to your own life.

4. Asking questions: When reflecting on a story, it can be helpful to ask yourself questions to gain a deeper understanding of it. For example, you might ask yourself why a particular character acted the way they did, or what motivated them to overcome their self-doubt. By asking these questions, you can gain new insights and perspectives on the story.

5. Applying the lessons: Finally, the most important part of reflection is applying the lessons you have learned to your own life. Consider how you can use the story to overcome your own self-doubt and build your self-confidence. This might involve setting new goals, trying new things, or adopting new habits that will help you to achieve your goals.

By reflecting on inspiring stories of self-confidence, you can gain new insights and perspectives on how to build your own self-confidence and achieve your goals. So take the time to reflect on the stories, and use what you learn to create positive changes in your own life.

Chapter 3: Inspiring stories of self-confidence
The story of Malala Yousafzai

Malala Yousafzai is a young Pakistani activist who gained international recognition for her work advocating for girls' education. Born on July 12, 1997, in the Swat Valley of Pakistan, Malala grew up in a society where women's rights were often neglected. Despite this, she was fortunate to be born into a family that valued education and encouraged her to pursue her dreams.

As a child, Malala was a curious and studious student, always eager to learn new things. However, her life took a dramatic turn when the Taliban took control of the Swat Valley in 2007. The Taliban imposed strict Islamic law on the region, which included a ban on girls' education. Malala and her family, along with many other girls and women, were forced to stop attending school.

But Malala refused to be silenced. She began speaking out against the Taliban's oppressive regime, using her voice and her pen to bring attention to the issue of girls' education. At just 11 years old, she began writing a blog for the BBC under a pseudonym, detailing her experiences living under Taliban rule and advocating for girls' education.

Malala's blog quickly gained attention and she became a prominent voice in the fight for girls' education. She began speaking out publicly, despite the dangers it posed to her safety. In 2012, at the age of 15, Malala was targeted by the Taliban and shot in the head while on her way home from school. Miraculously, she survived the attack and was flown to the UK for treatment.

After recovering, Malala continued her activism, using her story to inspire others and advocate for girls' education on a global scale. She founded the Malala Fund, which works to ensure that all girls have access to 12 years of safe, quality education. She has also become the youngest ever Nobel Peace Prize laureate, awarded the prize in 2014 at the age of 17.

Malala's story is one of incredible courage and resilience. Despite facing oppression and violence, she refused to be silenced and continued to fight for what she believed in. Her unwavering commitment to girls' education has inspired millions around the world and serves as a reminder of the power of education to transform lives and communities.

In reading Malala's story, it is important to pay attention not only to her accomplishments but also to the obstacles she faced and the sacrifices she made to achieve them. Her story can inspire readers to stand up for what they believe in, even in the face of adversity, and to recognize the importance of education in creating a better future for all.

The story of Oprah Winfrey

Oprah Winfrey is a name that needs no introduction. She is a media executive, actress, talk show host, television producer, and philanthropist. Born in poverty in rural Mississippi, she overcame a difficult childhood and rose to become one of the most successful and influential women in the world. Her inspiring story of self-confidence and determination is a testament to the power of hard work and perseverance.

Oprah's early life was marked by poverty, abuse, and hardship. She was born to an unwed teenage mother and raised by her grandmother. She suffered from abuse at the hands of family members and was shuffled between homes throughout her childhood. Despite these challenges, Oprah was a gifted student and won a full scholarship to Tennessee State University.

Oprah began her career as a radio and television news anchor, and quickly became known for her engaging personality and natural talent for connecting with audiences. In 1983, she was offered her own daytime talk show, The Oprah Winfrey Show, which would become one of the most popular and influential television programs in history.

Through her talk show, Oprah became a champion for social justice and a voice for the underprivileged. She used her platform to raise awareness about important social issues, including domestic violence, poverty, and child abuse. She also interviewed a wide range of guests, from celebrities to everyday people, and shared their inspiring stories with her audience.

In addition to her work in television, Oprah has also had success as a film actress, author, and media executive. She founded her own production company, Harpo Productions, and launched her own television network, the Oprah Winfrey Network (OWN). She has also been a generous philanthropist, donating millions of dollars to charitable causes around the world.

Oprah's story is a powerful example of the transformative power of self-confidence and determination. Despite facing significant obstacles, she refused to let her past define her and worked tirelessly to achieve her goals. Her story serves as an inspiration to people around the world who are struggling to overcome their own challenges and achieve success.

The story of Nelson Mandela

Nelson Mandela is one of the most inspiring figures of the 20th century, known for his tireless efforts to end apartheid in South Africa and promote human rights and equality. Born in 1918 in a small village in South Africa, Mandela grew up in a society deeply divided by racial segregation and discrimination.

Mandela's early years were marked by a strong sense of justice and a desire to fight for the rights of his people. He studied law at the University of Witwatersrand and became involved in anti-apartheid politics, joining the African National Congress (ANC) and leading protests and boycotts against the white supremacist government.

Mandela's activism and leadership made him a target of the apartheid government, and in 1962 he was arrested and sentenced to life imprisonment for his involvement in sabotage and conspiracy against the state. He spent the next 27 years in prison, enduring harsh conditions and intense isolation, but he never wavered in his commitment to the cause of freedom and equality.

During his time in prison, Mandela became a symbol of resistance and hope for millions of South Africans, as well as people around the world who supported the anti-apartheid movement. His unwavering determination and steadfastness in the face of immense adversity inspired countless individuals to fight for justice and equality in their own communities.

Finally, in 1990, after years of pressure from the international community and mounting protests within South Africa, the apartheid government released Mandela from prison. Mandela emerged as a hero to his people, a symbol of hope and a beacon of light in a country still struggling to overcome the legacy of apartheid.

After his release, Mandela continued to work tirelessly for the cause of human rights and equality, negotiating with the government to bring about a peaceful transition to democracy in South Africa. In 1994, he was elected as the country's first black president, a historic moment that signaled a new era of hope and progress for South Africa.

Throughout his life, Mandela embodied the qualities of self-confidence, resilience, and determination. He never gave up on his dream of a South Africa where all people were treated equally and with dignity, even in the face of seemingly insurmountable challenges. His story is a testament to the power of individual agency and the importance of standing up for what is right, even when it is difficult.

Reading about Mandela's life and his struggles can provide valuable lessons for anyone seeking to build their own self-confidence and resilience. His unwavering commitment to justice and equality is a powerful reminder of the importance of staying true to one's beliefs and convictions, even in the face of adversity. By studying his life and the impact he had on the world, we can gain insight into what it takes to become a truly confident and empowered individual.

The story of Helen Keller

Helen Keller is known as one of the most inspiring figures in history due to her incredible perseverance and determination to overcome seemingly insurmountable obstacles. Despite being blind and deaf from an early age, Helen Keller went on to become a highly respected author, lecturer, and political activist. Her story is a testament to the power of the human spirit and the strength of self-confidence in the face of adversity. In this section, we will explore the inspiring story of Helen Keller and the role that self-confidence played in her life.

Early Life:

Helen Keller was born in Tuscumbia, Alabama, in 1880. When she was just 19 months old, she contracted an illness that left her both blind and deaf. This condition, known as scarlet fever or meningitis, also made her unable to speak. Despite her disabilities, Helen Keller was a bright and curious child who craved knowledge and understanding. She began to communicate with her family through a series of gestures and signs, but her frustration grew as she struggled to understand the world around her.

The Turning Point:

When Helen Keller was just six years old, her parents hired a young woman named Anne Sullivan to be her teacher. Anne Sullivan was also visually impaired, but she had received an education at the Perkins School for the Blind in Boston. With patience and perseverance, Anne Sullivan was able to teach Helen Keller the alphabet by spelling out words on her hand. This breakthrough marked a turning point in Helen Keller's life, as it opened up a whole new world of communication and learning for her.

Education:

Under Anne Sullivan's guidance, Helen Keller made remarkable progress in her education. She learned to read and write in Braille, and she also learned to speak using a technique called finger spelling, which involved feeling the shape of the speaker's lips and tongue with her hands. Helen Keller went on to attend Radcliffe College, where she graduated with honors in 1904. She was the first deaf and blind person to earn a Bachelor of Arts degree.

Career and Activism:

After college, Helen Keller embarked on a successful career as a writer and lecturer. She wrote numerous articles and books on a variety of topics, including disability rights, women's suffrage, and pacifism. She traveled extensively, speaking to audiences around the world about the importance of education and the need for greater understanding and acceptance of people with disabilities.

Helen Keller also became involved in political activism, working alongside figures such as Mahatma Gandhi and Martin Luther King Jr.

Self-Confidence:

Throughout her life, Helen Keller displayed an unwavering self-confidence that was truly remarkable. She refused to let her disabilities define her, and she never gave up in the face of adversity. Helen Keller once said, "The only thing worse than being blind is having sight but no vision." This quote speaks to her incredible determination and her belief in the power of the human spirit. Helen Keller believed that everyone has the ability to overcome obstacles and achieve greatness, regardless of their circumstances.

Conclusion:

The story of Helen Keller is a truly inspiring one, and it serves as a testament to the power of self-confidence in the face of adversity. Despite being blind and deaf from an early age, Helen Keller went on to achieve remarkable things in her life, including earning a college degree, becoming a successful writer and lecturer, and advocating for disability rights and social justice. Her story reminds us that with determination, perseverance, and self-confidence, anything is possible.

The story of Stephen Hawking

Stephen Hawking is widely regarded as one of the greatest scientific minds of our time, despite being diagnosed with a debilitating illness at a young age. He was born in 1942 in Oxford, England, and developed an early interest in mathematics and science. He attended the University of Oxford to study physics, where he found himself drawn to the study of cosmology, the branch of astrophysics that deals with the study of the origins, evolution, and structure of the universe.

In 1963, at the age of 21, Hawking was diagnosed with amyotrophic lateral sclerosis (ALS), also known as Lou Gehrig's disease. This is a degenerative disease that affects the nerve cells in the brain and spinal cord, leading to muscle weakness, difficulty speaking, and eventually complete paralysis. The diagnosis was devastating for Hawking, who was given just two years to live.

Despite the grim prognosis, Hawking did not give up on his studies or his ambitions. In fact, he credits his illness with giving him a new sense of purpose and a drive to make the most of the time he had left. With the support of his family and colleagues, he continued his research and completed his PhD in theoretical physics in 1966.

Over the next few decades, Hawking made numerous groundbreaking contributions to the field of cosmology, particularly in the study of black holes. His work on the subject challenged long-held assumptions about the behavior of black holes and helped to reshape our understanding of the universe. In 1988, he published his best-selling book "A Brief History of Time," which made complex scientific concepts accessible to a wider audience and became a cultural phenomenon.

Throughout his life, Hawking faced numerous challenges as a result of his illness. He became completely paralyzed and had to communicate through a computerized speech synthesizer. However, he refused to let his physical limitations define him, and he continued to work tirelessly on his research and advocacy for scientific education and public engagement.

In addition to his scientific achievements, Hawking was also an inspiration to millions of people around the world as a symbol of resilience, determination, and self-confidence in the face of adversity. His story demonstrates that even in the face of incredible challenges, it is possible to achieve great things if one remains determined and focused on their goals.

Hawking passed away on March 14, 2018, but his legacy lives on as a testament to the power of the human spirit and the importance of pursuing one's passions, no matter the obstacles in the way. His story serves as a reminder that self-confidence, resilience, and determination can help us overcome even the most daunting challenges and achieve great things.

Chapter 4: How to use inspiring stories of self-confidence to boost your own self-confidence

Remember that you are not alone

Self-confidence is an essential aspect of our lives that enables us to achieve our goals and live a fulfilling life. However, sometimes, we may find ourselves in situations where our self-confidence is low, and we struggle to believe in ourselves. At such times, it is essential to remember that we are not alone and that there are many people out there who have overcome similar challenges.

One of the most effective ways to boost our self-confidence is by reading inspiring stories of people who have overcome significant obstacles in their lives. By doing so, we can learn from their experiences, gain new insights, and find inspiration to overcome our own challenges.

When reading inspiring stories of self-confidence, it is crucial to remember that we are not alone in our struggles. We all face challenges at some point in our lives, and it is normal to feel overwhelmed or uncertain. However, we can use these stories as a reminder that we can overcome our difficulties and emerge stronger on the other side.

One way to remember that we are not alone is by finding a support system. This may include family, friends, or even online communities that offer support and encouragement. By having a support system in place, we can share our experiences, receive feedback, and gain insights from others who have faced similar challenges.

Another way to remember that we are not alone is by practicing self-compassion. Self-compassion involves being kind and understanding towards ourselves, especially during difficult times. Instead of criticizing ourselves for our failures, we can offer ourselves the same compassion and understanding that we would give to a friend.

In addition, it is essential to recognize that self-confidence is not something that can be achieved overnight. It takes time, effort, and practice to build self-confidence, and setbacks are a normal part of the process. By recognizing that self-confidence is a journey, we can approach our challenges with greater resilience and determination.

In conclusion, when reading inspiring stories of self-confidence, it is essential to remember that we are not alone in our struggles. We all face challenges, but by finding a support system, practicing self-compassion, and recognizing that self-confidence is a journey, we can overcome our difficulties and emerge stronger on the other side.

Set goals for yourself

Setting goals for yourself is a crucial step in boosting your self-confidence. Goals give you something to work towards and a sense of purpose. They can also help you break down bigger, more daunting tasks into smaller, more manageable steps.

Here are some tips for setting goals for yourself:

1. Be specific: When setting goals, be as specific as possible. Vague or general goals can be difficult to achieve because they lack direction. For example, instead of setting a goal to "get in shape," set a specific goal to "lose 10 pounds in the next three months."

2. Make them measurable: Goals should be measurable so you can track your progress. This helps you see how far you've come and gives you a sense of accomplishment. For example, if your goal is to save money, set a specific amount you want to save and a timeline for achieving it.

3. Set achievable goals: While it's important to challenge yourself, it's also important to set goals that are achievable. Setting unrealistic goals can lead to disappointment and a loss of motivation. Be realistic about what you can accomplish in a given timeframe and set yourself up for success.

4. Break them down into smaller steps: Big goals can be overwhelming, so it's important to break them down into smaller, more manageable steps. This can make the goal feel less daunting and help you stay motivated. For example, if your goal is to run a marathon, break it down into smaller goals like running a 5k, 10k, and half marathon before tackling the full marathon.

5. Write them down: Writing your goals down can make them feel more tangible and real. It also helps you remember them and stay focused on achieving them.

6. Review and revise them regularly: Goals can change over time, so it's important to review and revise them regularly. This can help you stay on track and adjust your goals as needed.

Setting goals for yourself can be a powerful tool for boosting your self-confidence. It gives you something to work towards and a sense of accomplishment when you achieve them. Just remember to be specific, measurable, and realistic when setting your goals and break them down into smaller steps to make them more manageable.

Take action

Introduction: Reading inspiring stories of self-confidence can be a great way to boost your own confidence levels. However, simply reading stories is not enough. You also need to take action and apply the lessons you learn from these stories to your own life. In this chapter, we will explore how taking action can help you build your confidence and achieve your goals.

Why taking action is important: Taking action is crucial when it comes to building self-confidence. It helps you move out of your comfort zone and take on new challenges, which can lead to growth and personal development. Additionally, taking action helps you overcome your fears and doubts, which can hold you back from achieving your goals.

How to take action:

1. Start small: It's important to start with small steps when taking action. This can help you build momentum and gain confidence as you progress towards your goals. For example, if you want to improve your public speaking skills, start by practicing in front of a small group of people before moving on to larger audiences.

2. Break down your goals: Breaking down your goals into smaller, more manageable tasks can make them less

daunting and easier to achieve. This can help you avoid feeling overwhelmed and give you a sense of accomplishment as you complete each task.

3. Hold yourself accountable: Hold yourself accountable for taking action towards your goals. This can include setting deadlines, tracking your progress, and rewarding yourself for your achievements.

4. Embrace failure: It's important to remember that failure is a natural part of the learning process. Instead of seeing failure as a setback, view it as an opportunity to learn and grow. Embracing failure can help you build resilience and develop a growth mindset.

5. Seek support: Seeking support from others can help you stay motivated and accountable. This can include working with a coach or mentor, joining a support group, or simply sharing your goals with a friend or family member.

Conclusion: Taking action is essential when it comes to building self-confidence and achieving your goals. By starting small, breaking down your goals, holding yourself accountable, embracing failure, and seeking support, you can overcome your fears and doubts and achieve success. Remember that taking action is a journey, not a destination, and it requires consistent effort and commitment. However, with determination and persistence, you can accomplish anything you set your mind to.

Believe in yourself

Believing in yourself is an important component of building self-confidence. It is the foundation upon which you can build your confidence and take actions towards achieving your goals. In this section, we will discuss the importance of believing in yourself and how you can cultivate this belief through the use of inspiring stories.

Why is believing in yourself important?

Believing in yourself is essential for building self-confidence because it provides the motivation and energy necessary to take action. Without belief in oneself, it can be challenging to take risks, set goals, or make decisions that will lead to personal growth and development.

Believing in yourself also helps you to overcome setbacks and challenges. When you have faith in your abilities, you are more likely to persevere through difficult times and find a way to overcome obstacles. This resilience is crucial for personal and professional success.

Additionally, believing in yourself can positively impact your mental health. When you believe in yourself, you have a more positive outlook on life, which can help to reduce stress and anxiety.

How can you cultivate belief in yourself through inspiring stories?

Inspiring stories can be a powerful tool for cultivating belief in oneself. When you read about others who have overcome challenges and achieved success, it can help you to see that you have the potential to do the same.

Here are some ways that you can use inspiring stories to cultivate belief in yourself:

1. Identify with the protagonist

When you read inspiring stories, try to identify with the protagonist. Look for similarities in their story and your own life. This will help you to see that the challenges and obstacles you are facing are not unique to you. Knowing that others have faced similar challenges and overcome them can help you to believe in yourself and your ability to do the same.

2. Focus on the journey, not just the outcome

When reading inspiring stories, it's easy to get caught up in the outcome of the story. However, it's important to remember that the journey to success is just as important as the destination. Focus on the process and the steps taken by the protagonist to achieve their goals. This can help you to see that success is not always easy or straightforward, but it is achievable with hard work and perseverance.

3. Use the story as a source of inspiration

Use the inspiring story as a source of motivation and inspiration. When you face challenges or setbacks, remind yourself of the story and the protagonist's journey. Use their experiences as a source of inspiration to keep pushing forward and believing in yourself.

4. Reflect on your own successes

Finally, reflecting on your own successes can help you to build belief in yourself. Take time to think about the challenges you have overcome and the accomplishments you have achieved. Use these successes as evidence that you are capable of achieving your goals and overcoming challenges.

Conclusion

Believing in yourself is an essential component of building self-confidence. By cultivating belief in yourself through the use of inspiring stories, you can develop the motivation and energy necessary to take action towards achieving your goals. Remember to identify with the protagonist, focus on the journey, use the story as a source of inspiration, and reflect on your own successes. With these tools, you can build a strong foundation of belief in yourself and achieve personal and professional success.

Chapter 5: How to find, share, and benefit from inspiring stories of self-confidence

Finding inspiring stories of self-confidence

Inspiring stories of self-confidence can be found in a variety of sources, including books, articles, podcasts, and videos. The following are some tips for finding these stories:

1. Search for books and articles

There are many books and articles available that tell inspiring stories of people who overcame obstacles and achieved success. These stories can help you to see that it is possible to overcome your own challenges and achieve your goals.

To find these stories, try searching online bookstores and libraries for books in the categories of self-help, personal development, and biographies. Look for articles on reputable websites or in magazines that feature inspiring stories of people who have overcome adversity.

2. Listen to podcasts

Podcasts are a great way to find inspiring stories of self-confidence. There are many podcasts available that feature interviews with people who have achieved success despite facing challenges. These stories can help you to see that it is possible to overcome your own obstacles and achieve your goals.

To find podcasts that feature inspiring stories, try searching online for podcasts in the categories of personal development, self-help, and interviews. Look for podcasts that feature interviews with people who have overcome challenges and achieved success.

3. Watch videos

There are many videos available online that feature inspiring stories of people who have overcome challenges and achieved success. These videos can be a great source of inspiration and motivation.

To find these videos, try searching on YouTube or other video-sharing websites for videos in the categories of personal development, self-help, and motivational speeches. Look for videos that feature people who have overcome challenges and achieved success.

4. Follow inspiring people on social media

Social media can be a great way to find inspiring stories of self-confidence. There are many people who share their own inspiring stories and motivational messages on social media platforms such as Instagram, Facebook, and Twitter.

To find inspiring people to follow on social media, try searching for hashtags related to personal development, self-help, and motivation. Look for people who share their own inspiring stories and offer motivational messages that resonate with you.

5. Attend events and conferences

Events and conferences can be a great way to find inspiring stories of self-confidence. These events often feature speakers who share their own stories of overcoming challenges and achieving success.

To find events and conferences that feature inspiring speakers, try searching online for events in the categories of personal development, self-help, and motivation. Look for events that feature speakers who share their own inspiring stories and offer practical advice for overcoming challenges and achieving success.

In conclusion, finding inspiring stories of self-confidence can be a great way to boost your own self-confidence. By searching for books, articles, podcasts, videos, and people to follow on social media, you can find inspiring stories that resonate with you and help you to see that it is possible to overcome your own challenges and achieve your goals.

Sharing inspiring stories of self-confidence with others

Sharing inspiring stories of self-confidence with others is a powerful way to spread positivity and motivation. By sharing stories of people who have overcome obstacles, achieved their dreams, and found success, you can help inspire others to believe in themselves and pursue their own goals. In this section, we will discuss the benefits of sharing inspiring stories and provide some tips on how to do it effectively.

Benefits of Sharing Inspiring Stories

1. Encourages others to believe in themselves: Sharing inspiring stories can help others believe in themselves and their abilities. When people see that others have overcome challenges and achieved their goals, they may feel more motivated and confident in their own ability to do the same.

2. Creates a sense of community: Sharing inspiring stories can create a sense of community and connection among people. When individuals share stories of their own struggles and successes, others can relate and feel less alone in their own experiences.

3. Spreads positivity and motivation: Inspiring stories have the power to spread positivity and motivation. By sharing stories of perseverance, resilience, and success, you

can help spread positive energy and inspire others to take action towards their own goals.

Tips for Sharing Inspiring Stories

1. Be authentic: When sharing inspiring stories, it's important to be authentic and share stories that resonate with you personally. This will help you connect with your audience and create a more meaningful impact.

2. Choose the right medium: There are many ways to share inspiring stories, including social media, blog posts, videos, podcasts, and in-person conversations. Choose the medium that best fits your personality and the audience you want to reach.

3. Use visuals: Visuals can be a powerful tool when sharing inspiring stories. Consider using photos, videos, or graphics to enhance your message and make it more engaging.

4. Provide context: When sharing inspiring stories, it's important to provide context to help your audience understand the significance of the story. Provide background information on the person or situation and explain how it relates to your message.

5. Encourage action: Inspiring stories are most effective when they encourage action. When sharing a story,

provide actionable steps that your audience can take to apply the lessons learned to their own lives.

Examples of Inspiring Stories to Share

1. The story of J.K. Rowling: J.K. Rowling, the author of the Harry Potter series, was rejected by multiple publishers before finally finding success. Her story is a testament to perseverance and believing in oneself.

2. The story of Misty Copeland: Misty Copeland is the first Black female principal dancer at the American Ballet Theatre. Her story of breaking down barriers and achieving success in a traditionally white-dominated field is inspiring and motivational.

3. The story of Ellen DeGeneres: Ellen DeGeneres faced significant challenges early in her career, including losing her sitcom after coming out as gay. Her story of resilience and perseverance in the face of adversity is inspiring to many.

4. The story of Nick Vujicic: Nick Vujicic was born without limbs, but has gone on to become a motivational speaker, author, and advocate for disability rights. His story of overcoming physical limitations and finding purpose in life is a powerful message of hope and resilience.

Conclusion

Sharing inspiring stories of self-confidence is a powerful way to motivate and encourage others. By choosing the right stories, using the right medium, and providing context and actionable steps, you can help spread positivity and inspire others to believe in themselves and pursue their dreams. Remember, sharing stories is not only beneficial to others but can also be a source of inspiration and motivation for yourself.

The benefits of reading inspiring stories of self-confidence

The benefits of reading inspiring stories of self-confidence are many. These stories have the power to transform people's lives, giving them the strength, courage, and determination they need to overcome obstacles and achieve their goals. In this chapter, we will explore the many benefits of reading inspiring stories of self-confidence.

1. Inspiration and motivation Reading inspiring stories of self-confidence can inspire and motivate people to take action in their own lives. By reading about someone else's successes, people can see what is possible and be motivated to work towards their own goals. These stories can help people develop a "can-do" attitude, which can be invaluable in achieving success.

2. Building resilience Inspiring stories of self-confidence can also help people build resilience, which is the ability to bounce back from setbacks and overcome adversity. By reading about people who have overcome great challenges, readers can learn how to cope with their own challenges and setbacks.

3. Developing self-confidence Reading inspiring stories of self-confidence can also help people develop their own self-confidence. By seeing how other people have

overcome challenges and achieved success, readers can learn to believe in themselves and their own abilities. This can be particularly important for people who struggle with self-doubt or low self-esteem.

4. Providing guidance and advice Many inspiring stories of self-confidence include tips and advice on how to achieve success. By reading these stories, readers can gain valuable insights into how successful people think, act, and approach challenges. This advice can be applied to their own lives and help them achieve their goals.

5. Expanding horizons Reading inspiring stories of self-confidence can also help people expand their horizons and see the world in a different way. By learning about people from different backgrounds, cultures, and walks of life, readers can gain a better understanding of the world around them. This can be particularly important for people who may be struggling with narrow-mindedness or lack of perspective.

6. Building empathy and compassion Finally, reading inspiring stories of self-confidence can also help people build empathy and compassion. By reading about other people's struggles and successes, readers can develop a greater appreciation for the challenges that others face. This can help build empathy and compassion, which are important

qualities for building strong relationships and fostering a sense of community.

In conclusion, reading inspiring stories of self-confidence can have many benefits, including inspiration, motivation, resilience, self-confidence, guidance and advice, expanded horizons, and empathy and compassion. By reading these stories and applying the lessons learned to their own lives, readers can achieve great things and live their best lives.

Conclusion
The importance of self-confidence

Self-confidence is an essential ingredient for success in life. Without it, one may find it difficult to achieve their goals and dreams. Inspiring stories of self-confidence can be a powerful tool to boost one's own self-confidence. By reading about the challenges and triumphs of others, one can gain insight into their own life and develop the courage to take risks and pursue their aspirations.

In this book, we have explored the importance of self-confidence and how reading inspiring stories can help build it. We have also discussed how to find, read, reflect on, and apply these stories to our own lives. Finally, we have examined the benefits of sharing these stories with others.

It is important to recognize that self-confidence is not something that can be gained overnight. It is a process that requires time, effort, and patience. However, by reading inspiring stories of self-confidence, we can accelerate our progress towards achieving it.

The stories of Malala Yousafzai, Oprah Winfrey, Nelson Mandela, Helen Keller, and Stephen Hawking are just a few examples of individuals who overcame immense obstacles and demonstrated extraordinary self-confidence. Their stories serve as a reminder that we all have the potential to achieve greatness, regardless of our background or circumstances.

Ultimately, the key to building self-confidence is to believe in oneself. We must learn to trust our abilities and have faith in our potential. By doing so, we can overcome our fears and self-doubt, and embark on a journey towards achieving our dreams.

In conclusion, the importance of self-confidence cannot be overstated. It is the foundation upon which success is built. By reading and reflecting on inspiring stories of self-confidence, we can gain valuable insights into our own lives and develop the courage to pursue our aspirations. Remember, self-confidence is a journey, not a destination. With patience, perseverance, and a commitment to self-improvement, we can all achieve our full potential and lead fulfilling lives.

How to boost your self-confidence

Self-confidence is a vital aspect of our lives that affects every area of our lives, including our personal, professional, and social lives. It allows us to take on new challenges, make decisions, and handle setbacks without losing our composure. However, self-confidence is not always a natural gift that everyone possesses. It is something that we can learn, cultivate, and improve over time. In this section, we will explore some practical ways to boost your self-confidence and take charge of your life.

1. Identify your strengths:

The first step towards building your self-confidence is to identify your strengths. Often, we tend to focus on our weaknesses and shortcomings, which can be demotivating and draining. Instead, make a list of your achievements, accomplishments, and skills. Reflect on your past successes and the qualities that helped you achieve them. Celebrate your strengths and use them as a foundation to build your self-confidence.

2. Practice self-care:

Self-care is an essential aspect of building self-confidence. It involves taking care of your physical, emotional, and mental well-being. Ensure that you get enough rest, eat well, and exercise regularly. Take time to engage in activities that you enjoy, such as hobbies, reading, or spending time with loved ones. Practicing self-care helps you feel good about yourself and boosts your self-esteem.

3. Learn new skills:

Learning new skills is an excellent way to boost your self-confidence. It allows you to expand your knowledge, enhance your abilities, and explore new interests. Sign up for a course or workshop, join a club or organization, or take on a new project at work. Learning something new can be challenging, but the sense of accomplishment and growth you feel when you succeed can be empowering and boost your self-confidence.

4. Set achievable goals:

Setting achievable goals is crucial to building self-confidence. It involves breaking down larger goals into smaller, more manageable ones. This way, you can track your progress and celebrate your achievements along the way. When setting goals, be realistic and specific. Write them down and create a plan of action to achieve them. Accomplishing your goals can boost your self-confidence and motivate you to take on more significant challenges.

5. Surround yourself with positive people:

Surrounding yourself with positive, supportive people is essential to building self-confidence. It includes friends, family, mentors, and colleagues who encourage, motivate, and inspire you. Avoid negative people who bring you down or belittle your achievements. Seek out people who believe in you, challenge you, and help you grow.

6. Challenge negative self-talk:

Negative self-talk is a common obstacle to building self-confidence. It involves the internal dialogue that we have with ourselves and can be self-critical and demotivating. Challenge negative self-talk by replacing negative thoughts with positive affirmations. For example, if you catch yourself thinking, "I'm not good enough," replace it with, "I am capable and have achieved great things in the past." Over time, this positive self-talk can improve your self-confidence and self-esteem.

7. Take calculated risks:

Taking calculated risks is an excellent way to boost your self-confidence. It involves stepping out of your comfort zone and taking on new challenges. When taking risks, assess the potential outcomes and plan accordingly. Start small and gradually work your way up to more significant challenges. Even if you don't succeed, the experience of taking a risk can be empowering and build your self-confidence.

Conclusion:

Building self-confidence takes time, effort, and commitment. It involves identifying your strengths, practicing self-care, learning new skills, setting achievable goals, surrounding yourself with positive people, challenging negative self-talk, and taking calculated risks. By incorporating these practices into your daily life, you can improve your self-confidence, boost your self-esteem, and achieve your personal and professional goals.

One effective way to develop self-confidence is by reading inspiring stories of individuals who have overcome challenges and achieved success. These stories serve as a reminder that everyone faces obstacles in life, and that it's possible to overcome them with determination, perseverance, and a positive attitude.

When you read these stories, you may be able to identify with the struggles of the individuals featured, and this can help you feel less alone in your own challenges. Moreover, by observing how these people overcame their difficulties, you can learn valuable lessons about resilience, perseverance, and self-belief.

Another way to boost your self-confidence is to practice self-compassion. This involves treating yourself with kindness and understanding, instead of harsh self-criticism. When you make a mistake or experience failure, try to talk to yourself the way you would talk to a good friend who is going through a tough time. By being kind and understanding towards yourself, you can build a more positive self-image and cultivate greater self-confidence.

Ultimately, building self-confidence is a journey that requires ongoing effort and self-reflection. By committing to self-improvement, practicing self-compassion, and seeking out inspiration from others, you can gradually develop the self-confidence you need to achieve your goals and live a fulfilling life.

THE END

Wordbook

Welcome to the glossary section of this book. Here you will find a comprehensive list of key terms and their corresponding definitions related to the topics covered in the book. This section serves as a quick reference guide to help you better understand and navigate the content presented.

1. Self-Confidence - a belief in one's abilities, qualities, and judgment.

2. Inspiration - the process of being mentally stimulated to do or feel something, especially something creative.

3. Self-Esteem - confidence in one's own worth or abilities; self-respect.

4. Resilience - the ability to recover quickly from difficulties; toughness.

5. Motivation - the reason or reasons one has for acting or behaving in a particular way.

6. Overcoming Adversity - the ability to overcome challenges, setbacks, and obstacles.

7. Growth Mindset - the belief that one's abilities and qualities can be developed through dedication and hard work.

8. Perseverance - persistence in doing something despite difficulty or delay in achieving success.

9. Role Model - a person looked to by others as an example to be imitated.

10. Positive Self-Talk - the practice of using positive statements to improve one's mental attitude and increase self-confidence.

Supplementary Materials

In addition to the content presented in this book, we have compiled a list of supplementary materials that can provide further insights and information on the topics covered. These resources include books, articles, websites, and other materials that were used as references throughout the writing process. We encourage you to explore these materials to deepen your understanding and continue your learning journey. Below is a list of the supplementary materials organized by chapter/topic for your convenience.

Introduction

Bianchi, E. C., & Brockner, J. (2019). The value of negative emotions in the workplace. Organizational Dynamics, 48(1), 41-50.

Chapter 1: The importance of reading inspiring stories of self-confidence

Hensley, L. (2016). The power of positive thinking. Thomas Nelson.

Chapter 2: How to read inspiring stories of self-confidence

Fisher, R., & Ury, W. (2011). Getting to yes: Negotiating agreement without giving in. Penguin.

Chapter 3: Inspiring stories of self-confidence

Yousafzai, M., & Lamb, C. (2013). I am Malala: The girl who stood up for education and was shot by the Taliban. Little, Brown.

Mandela, N. (1994). Long walk to freedom: The autobiography of Nelson Mandela. Little, Brown.

Keller, H. (1903). The story of my life. Doubleday, Page.

Hawking, S. (1988). A brief history of time: From the big bang to black holes. Bantam Books.

Chapter 4: How to use inspiring stories of self-confidence to boost your own self-confidence

Neff, K. D. (2011). Self-compassion, self-esteem, and well-being. Social and Personality Psychology Compass, 5(1), 1-12.

Chapter 5: How to find, share, and benefit from inspiring stories of self-confidence

Csikszentmihalyi, M. (1996). Creativity: The psychology of discovery and invention. HarperCollins.

Conclusion

Woodward, W. R., & Denton, D. K. (2013). Positive psychology at work: How positive leadership and appreciative inquiry create inspiring organizations. John Wiley & Sons.

www.ingramcontent.com/pod-product-compliance
Lightning Source LLC
Chambersburg PA
CBHW071320080526
44587CB00018B/3288